Lookin' for Nessie!
A Kid's Guide To The Loch Ness, Scotland

Photography by John D. Weigand
Poetry by Penelope Dyan

Bellissima Publishing, LLC
Jamul, California
www.bellissimapublishing.com

Copyright © 2014 by Penny D. Weigand and John D. Weigand

All rights reserved. No part of this book may be reproduced or transmitted in any form or by any means, electronic or mechanical, including photocopying, recording, or by any other means, or by any information or storage retrieval system, without permission from the publisher.

ISBN 978-1-61477-139-5

First Edition

"It's not the towering sail,
but the unseen wind that moves the ship"

A Proverb

Lookin' For Nessie!
Bellissima Publishing, LLC

Introduction

Some claim the Loch Ness monster was first reported in 565 A.D. when, according to legend, St. Columba turned away a giant beast threatening a man in the Ness River that flows into the lake. No one knows if any of the stories and legends are true, and Nessie isn't the only reported sighting of a lake monster; but it is more than likely safe to say Nessie is the most famous of them all! And she has captured the imaginations of adults and children alike. There have been photos of Nessie and descriptions have varied as to her appearance. Some people think she is a living dinosaur.

Award winning author, attorney and former teacher, Penelope Dyan, and photographer, John D. Weigand went in search of the illusive Nessi themselves. Unfortunately, they didn't find Nessi; however, they are determined to return to the Loch Ness again one day in pursuit of Nessie and for a more extended search.

In the meantime, they created this book just for kids, to help kids practice reading skills through word recognition, and word repetition and rhyme. This is one of two books they created for kids about the Loch Ness. (Be sure to read, "On The Loch! A Kid's Guide To Urquhart Castle." for even more reading. fun.) There is also a video on the Bellissimavideo YouTube channel to further enhance the fun of the learning process!

Lookin' For Nessie!
Bellissima Publishing, LLC

Lookin' For Nessie!
A Kid's Guide To The Loch Ness, Scotland

Photography by John D. Weigand
Poetry by Penelope Dyan

You go looking for Nessie,
out on the lake.
You are told,
"She is right here in the Loch Ness!
Now, make no mistake!"

You follow the signs.
Mom says,
"We'll get on a boat.
And through the Loch Ness
we will cruise and float."
Your camera is in your hands.
You will take a picture or two.
You wonder if Nessie is out there,
just waiting for you.

Off the boat you walk a long path.
Dad looks at you and starts to laugh.
He tells you that it is not true,
and that Nessie is only a myth
made up to get tourist dollars from you.
Mom says she doesn't know;
so along the path
(with your camera ready)
you continue to go.

Another path takes you here.
Mom says,
"Ahead is the Urquhart Castle, dear."
The castle ruins look
like a great place to hide.
You wonder if Nessie
(the Loch Ness monster)
will be crouching inside.

You climb some steps
that go up so high.
You wonder when you get there,
if you will touch the sky.
Maybe Nessie will be right up there,
taking in the crisp cool air.

She isn't lying beneath these trees, basking in the autumn breeze.

You have looked for miles around!
Dear old Nessie can't be found!

You spot her likeness up ahead!
Your heart races
and you feel some dread.
Then you are relieved
that this isn't the real thing,
even though deep in your soul,
you feel a slight sting.
You thought you wanted to, at least,
take a picture of the beast.
But you decide for now
you'll settle for this,
and from Mom and dad,
a hug and kiss.

You look and wonder if Nessie,
is inside that yellow house,
just hidden away,
waiting for YOU to come out and play.
You decide you COULD get
over your fear,
if you found out Nessie was friendly,
and that she lived HERE!

You go to the 'Loch Ness Centre
And Exhibition.'
After all, YOU are on a mission!
It is Nessie that YOU came to find,
and THAT is all that is on YOUR mind!

You discover you are not the only one,
and others will continue to look,
long after YOU are done!
You see a submarine right here,
and you learn people
have looked for Nessie
(even using this sub) year after year!
Where Nessie is and where she will
remain and be,
may be destined to remain
a big mystery!
Or Nessie may one day soon
open the door of her hidden cave wide,
and invite a kid like you inside!

Mom buys for you
a stuffed Nessie toy,
just perfect for a small girl or boy.
It's a great symbol for a kid like you
and it serves as a reminder
that dreams do come true.
Then you decide that it is no mistake,
that Nessie is somewhere
out on that lake.
You tell your mom,
"I can feel it deep inside,
that Nessie is out there!
She just wants to hide!
Maybe someday out of the night,
Nessie will step into the light."

"We can easily forgive a child who is afraid of the dark; the real tragedy of life is when men are afraid of the light."

Plato